Dear Parent:
Your child's love of reading starts here!

Every child learns to read in a different way and at his or her own speed. Some go back and forth between reading levels and read favorite books again and again. Others read through each level in order. You can help your young reader improve and become more confident by encouraging his or her own interests and abilities. From books your child reads with you to the first books he or she reads alone, there are I Can Read Books for every stage of reading:

SHARED READING
Basic language, word repetition, and whimsical illustrations, ideal for sharing with your emergent reader

BEGINNING READING
Short sentences, familiar words, and simple concepts for children eager to read on their own

READING WITH HELP
Engaging stories, longer sentences, and language play for developing readers

READING ALONE
Complex plots, challenging vocabulary, and high-interest topics for the independent reader

ADVANCED READING
Short paragraphs, chapters, and exciting themes for the perfect bridge to chapter books

I Can Read Books have introduced children to the joy of reading since 1957. Featuring award-winning authors and illustrators and a fabulous cast of beloved characters, I Can Read Books set the standard for beginning readers.

A lifetime of discovery begins with the magical words **"I Can Read!"**

Visit www.icanread.com for information
on enriching your child's reading experience.

I Can Read Book® is a trademark of HarperCollins Publishers.

Guinness World Records: Wacky Wheels
Copyright © 2016 Guinness World Records Limited.
Guinness World Records and related logos are trademarks of Guinness World Records Limited.
All records and information accurate as of February 1, 2015

Library of Congress Control Number: 2014959385
ISBN 978-0-06-234186-0 (trade bdg.)—ISBN 978-0-06-234185-3 (pbk.)
Book design by Victor Joseph Ochoa

15 16 17 18 19   SCP   10 9 8 7 6 5 4 3 2 1   ❖   First Edition

GUINNESS WORLD RECORDS

WACKY WHEELS

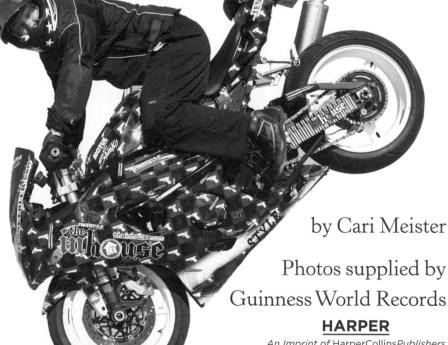

by Cari Meister

Photos supplied by
Guinness World Records

HARPER

An Imprint of HarperCollins*Publishers*

Bigfoot 5 is the **largest monster truck** in the world.

It is 15 feet, 6 inches tall.

Bigfoot 5 weighs 38,000 pounds.

The **largest skateboard** was created in 2009 by Rob Dyrdek and Joe Ciaglia for the MTV series *Rob Dyrdek's Fantasy Factory.* It is 36 feet, 7 inches long.

Didi Senft from Germany
holds the world record for building
the **largest rideable bicycle**.
Each of the bike's wheels
is almost 11 feet across!

Italian Fabio Reggiani built the **tallest rideable motorcycle**. At 16 feet, 8.78 inches high, it is five times taller than a regular motorcycle.

From the ground to the roof, the **tallest limo** in the world measures 10 feet, 11 inches. It has two engines

and took 4,000 hours to build.

Gary Duval, a theme park

ride designer from Australia,

came up with the idea.

The world record for the **heaviest limo** is held by Midnight Rider. It weighs in at a whopping 50,560 pounds!
The super-long car can carry up to 40 people.

The **largest land vehicle** weighs
31.3 million pounds,
is 722 feet long and 310 feet tall.
It is used by a German coal mine
to move dirt and coal.

What does a band do when there's no stage?
Build the **longest trike** that works as a movable grandstand!

That's what Swiss carnival group Guggä-Rugger Buus did in 2003. The trike is 26 feet, 7 inches long and can hold 21 band members on its stage.

Tilo and Wilfried Niebel built the **heaviest rideable motorcycle**. The beast, named Panzerbike, weighs 10,470 pounds! ("Panzer" means "tank" in German.)

Wouter van den Bosch,

a Dutch inventor,

created the **heaviest**

rideable tricycle in 2010.

It weighs 1,650 pounds!

A lot of golfers can fit aboard this 31-foot, 6.7-inch-long cart! Mike's Golf Carts in Georgia earned the world record for the **longest golf cart** in 2013.

David Weichenberger from Austria
set the record for
the **longest jump on a unicycle**.
He leaped 9 feet, 8 inches
on his unicycle in 2006.

The **lowest roadworthy car**

was built in 2010

by teachers and students in Japan.

It is 17.79 inches high.

The car is named Mirai.

"Mirai" means "future" in Japanese.
Most of the car's parts—
including the lights, frame,
and seat—were made
at Okayama Sanyo High School.

The **largest mining truck** has jumbo tires, a huge cab, and an enormous dumping bed. The bed can hold more than 890,667 pounds of coal!

This cozy trailer is the **smallest caravan** in the world.

It is 5 feet, 0.24 inches high;

2 feet, 7.9 inches wide;

and 7 feet, 10.9 inches long.

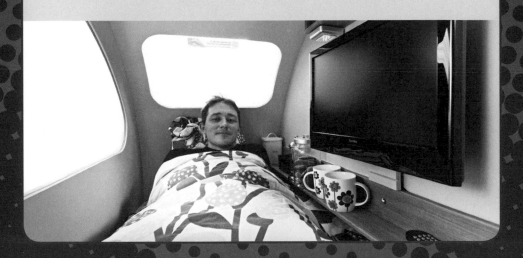

Gary Hatter set the record

for the **longest lawn mower ride**.

He rode his mower

for 260 days in a row.

Rain and snow did not stop him!

He drove through 48 states

and parts of Canada and Mexico.

Hatter traveled 14,594.5 miles.

His top speed?

Nine miles per hour (mph).

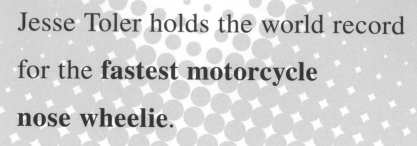

Jesse Toler holds the world record for the **fastest motorcycle nose wheelie**. Toler set his record by traveling at 150 mph.

Colin Furze built

the **fastest motorized stroller**

using a motorcycle engine.

The stroller's top recorded

speed was 53 mph.

Edd China set the record
for the **fastest toilet** in 2011.
Called the "Bog Standard,"
this vehicle includes a bathtub,
sink, and laundry basket,
and can travel at up to 42 mph.

The "Best Man" is the **fastest wedding chapel** on wheels. It has stained-glass windows, an organ, an altar, and two wooden pews. Its top speed is 62 mph.

The hair on the **hairiest car** is real!
It was combed, washed, and dyed.
The record was first set
with 220 pounds of hair.
Now the car has 265 pounds of hair!

In August 2013, Giuliano Casadei from the UK set the record for the **longest bumper car marathon**. He bumped for 26 hours, 51 minutes, and 8 seconds without stopping!

Built by Frederick Reifsteck,
the **largest motorized
shopping cart** in the world
is 27 feet long, 15 feet tall,
and 8 feet wide.

In a hurry? No time to shop?
You may need this shopping cart!
The **fastest motorized shopping cart**
was made by Matt McKeown.
It can go more than 70 mph.

The **loudest bike horn**
was made in England, UK, in 2013
and reaches 132.6 decibels.
That's about as loud as a plane
taking off nearby.